YOU
MUST NOT
FORGET

You Must Not Forget
© 2024 Catharine Day
All rights reserved.

Published by Day Inc.

Fort Worth, TX

For all the women
who nurture

IN LOVING MEMORY
Nana, Mary Snow
1932-2023

Contents

INTRODUCTION

Have you ever experienced something and thought, "I want to remember this forever"? Sadly, I've found that only a handful of these memories truly stay; the rest slip through the cracks. When I became a mother I started having more of these treasurable moments. Something about the solitude of motherhood, the slow pace, and the bouquet of new experiences awakened something in me. I didn't have the energy to keep a journal. So, I jotted my thoughts down in my notes during the day and revisited them later. These reflections became a lifeline in times of discouragement, helping me rediscover myself amidst my new identity as a mom. They stood as evidence that while my children were learning, growing, and having transformative experiences, I was too. My poems began with motherhood, but they helped reframe the rest of my life as well—my body, my home, my relationships, all of it. Our lives are constantly teaching us little lessons meant just for us—may we recognize them, learn from them, and, most importantly, may we never forget them.

PART ONE

NEW MOTHER

She is the same, but she is different.
She is different, but she is still the same.

NEW BODY

People say birth changes a woman's body. It's true.
Her heart will grow until it pushes against her ribcage,
filling her entire body cavity
the pressure creating a beautiful ache.
One arm strengthens while the other bends into a hook,
occupied for two years.
Feet begin acting as hands.
Shoulders become strong enough to carry a house.
And no, she won't "grow eyes in the back of her head."
That's wrong.
Every cell of her body will turn into eyes.
360 degrees of eye cells,
observing, sensing, watching,
a sentinel standing guard.

Doesn't she look great?

Yes, *because she is.*

MOTHER EARTH

The same earth that gives encouraging sunsets
also rains on wedding days.
The same earth that is home to horses and koalas
also breeds mosquitoes and fire ants.
The same earth that quakes so hard it breaks houses in half
also grows sweet cherry tomatoes in the backyard each summer.
The same earth that mercilessly floods
also superblooms wild flowers.

How can we love this earth?
How can we not?

AFTER BIRTH

Eat the fridge down to the bone.

This shirt is clean enough.

What time is it?

What day is it?

Sure, stop by.

Please don't kiss the baby.

I can't help but kiss the baby.

Who does she look more like?

I don't know,

she looks like a baby.

Oh, don't worry, we've got it.

The next day.

Please help.

How much did you tear?

Too much.

How long is your mom staying?

Not long enough.

My friend says it's just a season.

I agree.

A scary and beautiful season

like Halloween and Christmas had a baby.

NINE MONTHS PREGNANT

Go to the bathroom nine times a day,

pull leggings up eight times a day,

check calendar seven times a day,

recite due date six times a day,

complain about acid reflux five times a day,

eat a snack four times a day,

call mom three times a day,

get help up two times a day,

cry about something irrational once a day,

see toes, zero times a day.

CELESTIAL BEING

She went in as a full moon
and gave birth to a new star.

THE WILD

Life is twisty. Bumpy. Knotted mangled gnarled wild.

We try to organize it.

Tame it. Make it predictable. Cultivate it.

Put it into orderly little boxes.

Then something uncontrollable happens and breaks our boxes.

We shake our fist at the sky and say,

"This is wrong our world is broken!"

But then we remember

our Earth is not made of boxes.

It is made of bumpy, knotted, gnarled wild

and while we might prefer our boxes,

we were born to survive *the wild*.

WHEN ONE BECOMES TWO

You sleep on my chest and it feels right.
Like my body wasn't quite ready to give you up.
They say I cannot sleep with you.
So you sleep in a crib next door.
And as I toss and turn
the only logical explanation
for not being able to sleep
is that after nine months of sleeping with you,
I can't sleep without you.

SLEEP WHEN THEY SLEEP

I don't want to sleep.

I want to watch trash TV.
I want to go on a walk.
I want to online shop.
I want to sweep the kitchen.
I want to sit on the porch.
I want to take a bath.
I want to eat cake in silence.
I want to do nothing at all.

I want some time to be me.

NOT FOR YOU

My new boobs are
Large
Full
Soft
Round
Sassy
Bouncy
Tight
Seductive
Pillows
Too bad they shoot milk
like a loaded gun.

WORLDBUILDING

I put flowers on our table because

I want you to live in a beautiful world.

We have people over for Sunday dinner because

I want you to live in a friendly world.

I cook warm healthy meals because

I want you to live in an abundant world.

I play music and dance because

I want you to live in a happy world.

We pray together at night because

I want you to live in a hopeful world.

I kiss your cheeks and hold you close because

I want you to live in a loving world.

I can't control the world,

but I can control our world.

So while I can,

I'm going to make it

the best that I can.

NEW FRIEND

What will she think of my
house
our playroom
my child
my parenting
our marriage
where I picked to eat
how much I tip
my use of emojis
what snacks we buy
if we wear shoes inside
off-brand ziplocks

Having new friends is wonderful,
the cost of making them,
terrifying.

HAIR CONSPIRACY VOL I

Maybe the reason we lose our hair
after giving birth is because there's
no time to do anything with it.

HAIR CONSPIRACY VOL II

Maybe the reason we lose our hair
after giving birth is because they will
pull it all out anyway.

HEALTH

I don't know what's worse for your heart,
eating a whole stick of margarine or
reading the news.

WOMEN ARE GLUE

She sticks food to their bones
children to their schedules
curtains to the windows
messes to dust bins.
She sticks memories to walls
history to minds
compassion to hearts.
bottoms to piano benches
feet to safe paths
eyes to God.
She sticks.
And when she is gone,
She prays that it will hold.

THINGS I ASK GOOGLE

Squeaking sound during nursing normal?

Sleep schedule 4 mo old

How to help baby take bottle

Why doesn't baby sleep

Wake windows 7 mo old

How introduce solid food

When baby eat honey?

Play ideas 1 year old?

Toddler snack ideas healthy

Toddler throwing food

Sensory play ideas toddler

Toddler taking off own diaper

What age potty train

Toddler hitting

Age transition to toddler bed?

Toddler not staying in bed.

Best parenting books?

I don't know why I'm asking Google.

Google has never had a baby.

EVERYONE ELSE

Everyone else is fit

Everyone else travels

Everyone else has a clean house

Everyone else is creative

Everyone else is smart

Everyone else is is wearing a clean shirt

Everyone else is organized

Everyone else makes snack-art and Easter baskets.

But you don't want everyone else,

you only want me.

HORTICULTURE

Different places bring out different parts of myself.

In New York I walk fast and ask for the check.

I stay out late, wear lipstick, dream big, and eat pizza in the street.

In Hawaii I live simply, resting in warm sand.

I don't brush my hair, or know what time it is.

I sing like a bird.

In Italy I'm a lover.

In Canada I'm a kind zealot with swollen cankles.

In Washington I'm a thrifter stitching my identity together from scraps of things

and people that I love—held by the valley, the mountains, the safe arms of my mother.

In Texas I'm a cowgirl exploring the Wild West.

I ride bulls and wrangle my calves.

Here I am brave cultivating my life and building our homestead.

I used to ache for a place to let my taproot run deep.

But sometimes roots don't run deep,

sometimes roots spread wide and reach far,

and they grow just fine.

They grow just fine.

PAJAMA PARABLE

My children shed their pajamas like snake skins.

Layer by layer.

Their growth is imperceivable by me,

but made apparent by stretching cotton,

pulling seams,

little exposed ankles and wrists.

And so I go and get a new pair,

baggy,

generous,

"room to grow."

But deep down I know,

no matter how many sizes up I go,

one day they'll fit just right,

as I lean down,

to kiss them goodnight.

SIZES

xs/sm/med/lrg/xl

When I feel like I literally do not "fit in"
I remind myself, yes,
the world likes small things like diamonds and daisies,
and extra small things, like ladybugs and snowflakes
but it also likes large things like horses, swimming pools, and
grand pianos.
And extra large things, like the moon, the mountains, the ocean
and the opera.
And it likes everything in between, medium sized things like dogs,
cashmere sweaters, swing sets and bonfires.

The earth loves all sizes.
All sizes are good.

TIME OFF

It's an uneasy feeling
the dishwasher started
the house decently clean
one baby sleeping
the other playing by themselves
Can I play too?
No.
Ok.
Too early to start dinner
too late to run an errand
so I sit down
a stranger
to the stillness

WITH CHILD

They say people carry emotions in their body. I do.

But I also carry every lost child.

The girl snatched by the FedEx man.

The infant lost by placental abruption.

The baby who lived for only 24 hours.

The "late-term miscarriage"

that wasn't "a miscarriage." He was your son.

I carry them all in the spaces between my ribs,

and when I breathe it hurts.

And when all the spaces between my ribs are full

I will continue to carry them in my bones until my

marrow is replaced with sorrow.

I might be done having children,

but I will never be done carrying them.

TODDLER

Sweet boy,
small curious hands determined
to undo today's doings.

OCTOPUS MOM

An octopus will never meet its mother.
She dies after laying her eggs.
All her babies need to know she leaves for them in their DNA–
how to hunt, how to hide, how to transform.
The mother octopus doesn't raise her young,
 instead she resides in them–embedded in every cell.

MYSTERIES OF MOTHERHOOD

How it takes one hour to clean a house,

and only ten minutes to destroy it.

How do double strollers fit through doorways?

Having to wait for a doctor appointment... it's an appointment.

Where does all the money go?

How do babies breathe while breastfeeding?

Who invented apple squeezes,

and what did children eat before them?

Why is salad twice the cost but only half the calories?

How is it, one day there's not enough space to

fit one more thing in the fridge

and the next day

— it's empty?

LIONESSES

Three of my friends surprise me, announcing they are all pregnant.
"Why didn't you tell me we were having babies?!" I joke.
Later, I learn that the lionesses in a pride have their cubs at the
same time, so they can take turns hunting
and watching their young.
And then I realize—I wasn't joking.
Even a lioness knows,
it's too hard to raise a cub alone.

SOLO PLAY

She tiptoes around the house,

leaps past doorways,

moves in shadows.

holds her breath,

swallows her sneezes.

To be heard is to be hailed.

To be seen is to be needed.

SOFT PLACES

There's something so honoring when a baby
falls asleep in your arms — accepting you as a safe place to find rest.
I fondly reminisce of the soft safe places I have slept.
My best friend's suede couch after a day of swimming.
The soft carpet of my Nana's floor as she watches old drama pieces,
the sound of soup bubbling on the stove.

It is a beautiful feeling to find those places,
and it's an even more beautiful feeling to be that place
for others.

WALKING MOM

When I pass a mother pushing her stroller I think
I don't know you, but I know you.

I don't know where you're from,
if you work or what show you're binging.
But I do know everyday you channel your inner strength,
that this morning you've already calmed a crying child,
and said, "leave your shoes on" at least once.

I don't know if you're married, what grocery store you shop at
or if you prefer dark or milk chocolate.
But I do know your heart breaks when you read the news,
that you'd love an hour to yourself,
and that you cherish that little bundle in your stroller
so much you'd push it 1,000 miles and back if you had to.

We don't know each other,
But we know each other.

PART TWO

STAINS

At the end of the day
women get the stains out.
The blood.
The frosting.
The green knees dragged across the grass.
The pen.
The pain.
The memories turned mess.
We sing.
We scrub.
We hum.
We pat.
We rock.
Until it all lifts in the wash.
Until it is as good as new
—maybe even better.

A GOOD WOMAN

I've never tasted something she's made
and not loved it.
Not too much.
But nothing lacking.
I ask her for her secret and she shrugs like it's no secret,
anyone can do it.
She sends me the recipe later.
I keep it, treasure it, knowing it will never be quite the same.

Anna's coco
Maggie's rolls
Morgan's cookies
Hailey's salsa
Laurel's pie
Baylee's buttermilk syrup
Zoe's chocolate cake

I am made up of good women
and their recipe cards.

THE SCHEDULE

You wake up,
they're a newborn.
You make breakfast,
they're smiling.
You do the laundry,
they're crawling.
You call your friend,
they're eating solids.
You make lunch,
they're walking.
You do some chores,
they're saying "Mama."
You eat dinner,
they're leaving for college in the morning.

FORCED SMILE

Oh I'm so proud of you
for wiping your own nose.
I just wish you hadn't
used my curtains to do it.

HOW TO BE YOURSELF

First find some time to be alone.
Then find a patch of clean house to sit in.
Guard it.
Pretend you cannot hear the phone.
Or the little fists on the door.
Or the question, "Where's the laundry detergent?"
Then take off all the things that squeeze you,
jeans, bras, necklaces, even hair ties
and deep dive into yourself.
Leave the constructs, expectations, appointments, emails,
the schedules, podcasts, finances, and dirty breakfast plates
at the surface and swim below.
Down
Down
Down

Now you are alone — with yourself.
Wander with her, talk with her,
braid her hair, breathe together, encourage her,
hold her in your arms and tell her how proud you are of her,
listen to her —

her dreams, her disappointments,
revisit memories, plan a trip to Italy.
Take note of it all.

Then, when it's time to go,
promise her you will come back soon.

And then keep that promise.

CONSTRUCTION ZONE

Yes, our home might look like a construction zone.

Because it is.

Everyday we wake up and build.

We're building parents.

We're building children.

We're building our life.

Each night we tidy the construction site

each day it falls back into chaos.

We shift plans, knock down walls, and build new ones.

If we look like we don't know what we're doing,

it's because we don't.

This is the first time we've ever built anything like this.

We're figuring it out.

So please when you visit remember to duck under that beam.

Don't mind that pile of dishes.

Wade past the laundry room.

Step over that sandwich.

This is not a show home.

This is a construction zone.

TOMORROW

Tomorrow I will not eat popcorn for dinner.

I will call my friend.

I will fold the laundry.

I will brush my hair before going on a walk.

I will water the flowers.

I will go to the post office.

I will write in my journal.

I will get baking soda.

But not today,

tomorrow.

CONSPIRACY THEORY

Perhaps if we give her no help tending to her children
she will never have time or energy to leave her house
and scream in the streets in her "I've had it" voice that
things are very broken, and demand them to be fixed.

Yes, this is how we keep the streets quiet.

WOMAN

She said she would not get sick.
So she didn't.

BABY BURNOUT

On the hard days anything can break you.

Trying to remember which streaming platform

the show is on while your toddler impatiently pleads.

An egg falling out of the fridge breaking onto the floor.

Telemarketers calling again.

Stubbing your toe.

The stroller-release mechanism.

Your general lack of life plans, or strategy, or a coherent thought.

Your husband's sock.

The self-awareness you are complaining about a fortunate life.

Knowing you need help, being too tired to ask for it.

There's not one thing, it's everything.

It's everything.

Until it's THAT one thing.

THE WARNING

The only thing keeping this whole operation
together is this bra.
And at exactly 7:01 PM
it's coming off.

A MOTHER'S LOVE

I cannot tell you how much a mother loves a child.
I can only tell you when an orca calf dies
the mother orca keeps her deceased calf with her,
pushing the small body through the water with her for 12 days.
And I can tell you that elephants will carry their fallen calf with
them, taking turns as they pass the small body from one member
of the herd to another, the heaviness too much for one to carry —
too heavy for the strongest mammal on earth.

This is what I can tell you.

TWO CHILDREN

People ask how it is going from one to two.

And honestly I'll never figure it out.

You can't vacuum when it's naptime.

And you can't vacuum when it's not naptime.

When do you vacuum?

SAD EARTH

A baby cries when it is sick.
A plea for help.

But the earth can't cry
so it lights itself on fire turning the sky red
it sends 5,000 miles of toxic algae blooms
to cover the shores
it melts glaciers and drowns cities
it shakes and breaks like a toddler
knocking down blocks
it heats like a
blistering fever.

The earth can't cry,
but I can see her crying.

SOCKS

Every time
I find a
    tiny sock
left in an
                obscure
place in
my house I think of it
as a little

love note

     left

for

me to

           find.

DEAR SOPHIE

You do not need to "become something"
for me to love you.
You do not need to win awards,
play instruments,
or have a prestigious career.
You do not need to solve
complicated problems,
test the highest,
run the fastest,
or be the most liked
for my love.

I love you thoroughly,
completely and entirely,
today.

SECOND CHILD

My first child didn't like it when I sang,
So I didn't sing to my second.
My first child didn't like to draw,
So I didn't offer crayons to my second.
My first child refused tomatoes,
So I never offered them to my second.

I only just learned
my second child loves music,
drawing and tomatoes.

Who would have thought people
are different and children are too?

MATRIARCHY

One time in high school my friend's mom came down to get food
from the fridge wearing only her T-shirt and underwear.
Confident and unapologetic she stood bathed in the fridge light
casually exploring the contents of Tupperware. Who was this
kind of woman who did not hide her skin or apologize for her legs?
Who was this kind of woman whose cheeks did not flush red and
did not fly like a startled bird, but stood on her feet, in her skin, on
her legs.

They say not all heroes wear capes.
I would say, they don't wear *pants* either.

LOVE MATH

I often hear people say the more children someone has,
the more they must divide themselves,
but I don't think so.

Every person we love multiplies us.

PAY GAP

for Lindsey

Thank you for taking this job.

For seeing us at our worst,

and coming back the next day.

You are brave — waking a sleeping toddler

You are strong — denying a second cookie.

You are kind — kissing bruises and bonks.

Thank you for offering love,

when our toddler offers rage.

For cleaning up the messes,

and then cleaning them again.

I could never afford to pay you how much you deserve.

So at night I thank God for you in my prayers,

and ask him to shower you in blessings forever

to make up the difference.

COMMANDER IN CHIEF

What if only someone who had birthed, nursed,
and raised a soldier had the right to declare war?

BIBLICAL

There aren't many mothers mentioned in the Bible.

But then again, Jesus could have been a mother.

He had twelve children he brought everywhere.

He told stories.

He shared his bread and fish at the park.

He healed bonks and bruises.

He was unpaid.

Unsupported.

And wrongly judged.

Despite it all,

His love changed the world forever.

And so does ours.

SHOW AND TELL

I show you the garden and you show me a butterfly.
I show you the ocean and you show me a shell.
I show you the lake and you show me a bird.
I show you the park and you show me a stick.

I love showing you the world,
I love seeing what you find.

"SHE LET HERSELF GO"

When they say she let herself go.
What they don't realize is she didn't
let herself go.
She let them go.
She let go of their approval,
their expectations,
the scale on the counter,
the hunger.
She let it all go.
And then she held herself.
All of herself.
And she ate to be full
instead of to disappear.
And she lived to see
And not to be seen.

GUILTY PLEASURE

for Harlan

Scraped knee, stubbed toe,
injustice on the playground.
You run to me
crying, climbing into my arms,
melting into me.
I hold you close
closing my eyes,
smelling your hair.
Savoring it.
Grateful for this moment,
to be needed,
to get to hold you close
again.

THE GREAT RACE

We pass our children off
to one another like a baton.
I slump over in exhaustion at the end of my lap
as you take off at a sprint.
Inhale. Exhale.
I catch my breath just as you come
around the corner with
the crying baton.
I close my eyes,
reach my hand back
and get ready
to run again, grateful to be
running this race – with you.

POSITION ON HUGS

Hugs don't solve problems,
but they do keep them in perspective.

ROMANCE

I don't need grand gestures of love,
I just need you to close the bag of tortilla chips.

MY LOVE IS

My love is a trampoline park.
A book read four times.
A bowl of oats.
Clean grout.
Waiting on hold for 20 minutes.
A stack of little folded shirts.
Asking for a new balloon.
A pile of trimmed crusts.

My love will look different every day,
but I promise if you look close enough
you will find it.

SAFE KEEPING

When people say they've "lost themselves" I think,
What does that even mean, how can that happen?
And then today my husband asked me where the title to our house
was... and I couldn't find it.
I remember when we moved in I put it in the file cabinet, a fairly
reasonable place.
But then I thought "No, it is too important, we must put it in a
safer place."
So I buried it deep in the back, where no one could find it,
including myself.

I can tell you where the sunscreen is,
the paper clips,
the Easter eggs,
but the title to our home... not a clue.

And that is when it struck me, maybe that's how we lose ourselves.
Those big things about ourselves, our dreams, hopes and loves
are so important to us we hide them to protect them.
We tuck them away so deep, and so "safe" that no one can hurt
them, touch them, even ourselves,
and then we forget...

OPTICAL ILLUSIONS

Let's never make love while wearing socks.
Not only because it would make my legs look shorter,
but because I want to see you fully and be seen by you fully.

So, no socks.

DEAR BEAR

Thank you for always being there
for fearlessly being a catchall for runny noses,
sleeping in a chokehold,
and taking countless spins in the washing machine.

Thank you for never taking a vacation day,
and for sleeping on airport floors when you
come with us on our vacations.

Thank you for attending every meal
being a wingman for every playdate,
and for deescalating every tantrum.

I knew we were going to have a baby;
but I didn't know we would also have a bear.
I'm grateful we did
I couldn't imagine raising
this boy without you,
Bear.

BEHIND THE CURTAIN

I hope you don't stop believing in magic
when I tell you Santa,
The Easter Bunny,
and the Tooth Fairy aren't real.
That they are in reality…
just me.

Instead,
I hope you start seeing the real magic,
that when you love someone it transforms
life into something truly special.

NATURE SHOWS

After watching nature shows with my children I realize why I resist leaving them. In every episode a hungry mother animal goes to hunt. She must leave her soft babies unattended. The narrative cuts to predators hunting for those babies. No matter the species, there is always a predator. Thankfully, the mother always returns in the nick of time, teeth bared, growling, biting, drawing blood.

Date night, lunch with friends, a walk in the woods, a bath — I resist fulfilling my needs because something primal inside me says, when I leave, I'm risking my babies to the jackal, the red tail fox, the vulture. And unlike the nature shows... what if I don't get back in time?

WHAT IT'S LIKE BEING A WOMAN

Marketplace.

For sale. Sound machine $15

What if it's a man?

And he becomes obsessed with me?

And he wants my address?

And he messages me "hi" on all my accounts.

So I have to delete them.

And move.

But he never gives up.

And devotes a wall to unflattering clipped photos of me

And follows me at the grocery store.

Lucy has messaged you.

Exhale. That was close.

Here is my address.

I'll leave it on the porch.

Thank you…

for being a woman.

A MOTHER NOTICES

A mother notices
a bothersome tag in the seam
a piece of bark stuck in a shoe
jam in-between fingers
a sharp toenail
disappointment
loneliness
a right shoe on a left foot.
Anyone can recognize the big wins,
the heartbreaks.
But what makes a mother special
is her ability to see
everything else.

SOME DAYS

Some days being a mom feels like: Give. Give. Give. Give. Give.
Give. Give. Give. Give. Give. Give. Give. Give. Give. Give.
Give. Give. Give. Give. Give. Give. Give. Give. Give. Give.
Give. Give. Give. Give. Give. Give. Give. Give. Give. Give.
Give. Give. Give. Give. Give. Give. Give. Give. Give. Give.
Give. Give. Give. Give. Give. Give. Give. Give. Give. Give.
Give. Give. Give. Give. Give. Give. Give. Give. Give. Give.
Give. Give. Give. Give. Give. Give. Give. Give. Give. Give.
Give. Give. Give. Give. Give. Give. Give. Give. Give. Give.
Give. Give. Give. Give. Give. Give. Give. Give. Give. Give.
Give. Give. Give. Give. Give. Give. Give. Give. Give. Give.
Give. Give. Give. Give. Give. Give. Give. Give. Give. Give.
Give. Give. Give. Give. Give. Give. Give. Give. Give. Give.
Give. Give. Give. Give. Give. Give. Give. Give. Give. Give.
Give. Give. Give. Give. Give. Give. Give. Give. Give. Give.
Give. Give. Give. Give. Give. Give. Give. Give. Give. Give.
Give. Give. Give. Give. Give. Give. Give. Give. Give. Give.
Give. Give. Give. Give. Give. Give. Give. Give. Give. Give.
Give. Give. Give. Give. Give. Give. Give. Give. Give. Give.
Give. Give. Give. Give. Give. Give. Give. Give. Give. Give.
Give. Give. Give. Give. Give. Give. Give. Give. Give. Give.
Give. Give. Give. Give. Give. Give. Give. Give. Give. Give.
Give.

HONORABLE DECORATIONS

Drool marks on my sweater
dog sticker on my pant leg,
and a noodle dried to my sleeve.
These are the medals of
motherhood that I wear with pride.

A CASE FOR CHILDREN

When you crawl into bed there's
a triceratops there.
When you hear music, you dance.
You go to the park and swing.
You sing again, hold hands and celebrate holidays.
You hug ten times a day, walk slower, read stories, swim and eat
popsicles.
You go to the zoo and pet a sheep.
At dinner you talk about petting a sheep.
You rewatch the Aristocats
and at the grocery store
you get a balloon.

Yes, as a parent there are things you will miss out on
because you have children.
But there are many wonderful things you get to do
because you have children.

PART THREE

QUILTING

Women quilt.

We create masterpieces from fragments, somethings

from nothings.

Taking five minutes here, and a few scraps there

piecing them together to make something usable, something warm.

We hold up our quilts for each other and admire one another's

creations.

No two are the same.

Each one a relic.

Growing up we had six mismatched chairs at our kitchen table.

A quilted table.

We had packed sandwiches at the ski lodges, passed-down skis,

and handmade hats—a quilted Christmas.

We had quilted closets and delicious quilted dinners.

We don't need it all for life to be perfect.

We'll take what we have.

We'll stitch it together.

We will make it perfect.

SHE'S GONE WALKING

I just read a book about a young girl traveling across Arizona to settle a new territory.

She completely changed her life by just walking.

And isn't it just that simple, changing your life?

It's just walking.

Walking into the rooms you want to be in.

Having the courage to walk out of the ones you don't.

I get up in the morning and walk.

I'm practicing.

I'm remembering that I know how.

That it's easy.

Isn't it funny how it's the first thing we learn to do?

Maybe it's all we need to know.

OXYTOCIN

After birth a woman's body releases hormones
that cause her to forget the pain of labor,
the stretching,
the contracting,
the near brush with death.
I wonder if this same hormone is also released after every
hard phase we pass through.

The nausea phase.
The cracked nipple phase.
The night wakes phase.
The "No!" phase.
The food throwing phase.
The biting phase.
The potty training phase.

We go through it and a couple days later look back and think,
"Was it really that bad?"
Yes.
It was.
It was really and truly so hard.

But you made it through that phase
you can make it through this one.

So when your body goes and does its magic helping you forget
all the pain you've passed through, you must not forget.

You must not forget.

I AM NOT A CUT FLOWER AND NEITHER ARE YOU

I am not a cut flower and neither are you.

We will not bloom once and be placed in a vase –

adored until we wilt –

thrown out with soggy smelly stems.

We are perennials.

Blooming again and again, year after year.

Returning more abundantly than before.

Taking up space.

Gaining root.

Flourishing unapologetically.

Confidently taking seasons of rest

and seasons of glory.

There is no end to our beauty.

There is no end to our bloom.

CROCKPOT LIFE

First, you learn what a crockpot is.

Then someone gifts you one—college-bound or newlywed.

It sits, rent-free, in your cabinet for years

until one Sunday, you finally try it.

And then it hits you:

you want a crockpot life.

A life slow, unfussy, rich with flavor—

where time and herbs turn everything good,

even the hardest, meanest potato.

Warm broth whispers

that the whole is greater than the sum of its parts,

and that all you need to feel incredibly rich

are root vegetables.

YOUR JOY

I like small rocks and sticks.
I like watching trains
and spotting airplanes.
I like the garbage truck,
and apple squeezes.
I like the neighbor's dog,
small cars,
tupperware lids,
strawberry toothpaste,
and the kitchen faucet.

I like them
because you do.

NEWBORN CASSEROLE

1 16 oz pack of validation

8 oz of wondering how the delivery went

2 ripe birth stories

4 tbs gladness it is not you

1 tsp gladness it once was you

1/2 c thinking you should have done more

1/2 c thinking you barely had time to do this

3/4 c hoping they like mushrooms

Bake and doubt your meal choice
at 400° for 40-60 minutes

Garnish with a side hug, a compliment about the baby,
and a moment of self reflection if your family is really finished.

THINGS I STOPPED APOLOGIZING FOR WHEN I TURNED 30

Wearing makeup

Not wearing makeup

I will not be at the party

My thighs

The house is not clean

I did not call you back

Buying things

Not buying things

Throwing things away

Keeping things

Quitting

Not eating that

Eating that

Asking questions

Sitting down

Leg hair

Resting

HOLY HOUSE

I asked God if he wanted to come to our house.

No matching socks,

bath toys trailing down the hallway,

bursting closets,

and a growing pile of laundry in the corner.

He said,

A house of order is a house of God

but so is a house with a bird nest of mail,

a pile of laundry books slouching into a donation pile,

a house riddled with clothes and dishes

and mismatched Tupperware lids.

So I said,

Come on in.

ROSE BUSH

Rose bushes make it look easy.

Big stunning gorgeous blooms on the outside.

I almost forget the inside of a rose bush is a pokey gnarled mess.

Blooming is not an easy process. It's dangerous, it's pokey.

When things look beautiful do not forget the thorns.

When life gets thorny, do not forget to look for the blooms.

CAKE PLATE

When my friends move away,
they each take a piece of me with them.
Is that what it means to die?
To love so deeply,
that you give away every little part of yourself
until there's nothing left—
but in the most beautiful way.
Like an empty cake plate,
finished
satisfied
shared
enjoyed.

IMMUNE SYSTEM

The first person I saw living on the street after I gave birth, I cried.
Where was his mother? Was she worried?
Then I read the news.
Refugees swimming, buildings collapsing, Black boys being shot by
the police.
Someone's baby swimming, someone's baby covered in rubble,
someone's baby shot by the police.
I cried.
My body didn't just worry for my child, it worried for them all.
Felt for them all.
So after my son was born I got shingles.
Hot worried angry blisters on my face.
And after my daughter, my whole body ached — every joint in my
body, inflamed, angry.

I went to the doctor.

He told me with each baby your immune system changes
and suddenly it all made sense.

Why my friend is taking a social media break.
Why I hide under my heavy duvet in the heat of the summer.

Why I search for therapy and medication
but the only thing that my body responds to
is flying across the country to sit at my mother's
kitchen table to eat vine-ripe tomatoes together.

My body recognizes "illness" differently now,
and so do I.

So do I.

LAVENDER FIELDS

When life's gruff and your heart is calloused,
climb into a warm bath filled with lavender salts and soak
until the only thing you can think about is lavender fields.
Then scrub scrub scrub until your skin turn soft again,
until your heart turns soft again.

SPRING

Is there anything more hopeful than a budding tulip,
pushing the cold earth aside to rise?
Maybe this is why we must garden,
to witness the resilience of a pansy,
the confidence of a peony,
the tenacity of mint.
Maybe we run our hands through soil
to remember we too were made from dirt,
to remember we too were born to bloom.

WHEN I KNOW

When you bring me a cup of water.

Or kill a wasp.

When your hands find my back while you read.

When our baby cries and I feel you get out of bed.

When you kiss me, and then kiss me again.

When you say,

"Don't delete that picture."

"Yes, the doors are both locked."

"No, that will never happen to you."

"Don't throw that away."

"Here. Use mine."

You told me you loved me the other night ...

but I already knew.

BOSS LADY

Today I took a bath at noon.
Sometimes I do things just to prove
to myself that I'm in control of my life
and not the other way around.

SHE TREE

I love the fall.
The trees naked
having dropped their towels.
Flexing their trunks.
Branches reaching toward heaven
root to sky stretching beauty.
All summer she holds a million leaves,
clinging to her.
She feeds them.
She holds them back.
Their love creates a canopy of shade
for others to rest under.
But in the fall she lets it all go
and takes a season
to herself.

ON HOPE

For my mother

I like to remember how my mother
scraped the black off the toast,
iced back together broken cake layers,
cut the mold off the cheese,
and wiped dirt off of a fallen sandwich.
If she thought it would be ok,
it was.

*I'm grateful for
everyone who urged
me to create this
book. Thank you.
Your kind words
carried me forward.*

ACKNOWLEDGMENTS

I would like to thank my dear friend Jena Fox for being the first to read and provide feedback on my poems and for being a lifelong friend — I wouldn't be the person/writer I am today without your friendship. I would also like to thank Brenda Nelson and Meghan Truman for the nights spent with warm tea and talking about our projects — together we created a sacred space for this book to have a chance at existence. Thank you Chandler Holmes for always keeping me on track and my book club for cheering me on. To my husband Ryan — thank you for taking my dream seriously and structuring our lives to make my writing a possibility; above all thank you for your steadfast love. I would like to thank my Nana, Mary Snow, who always left enthusiastic Facebook comments on my poems and told me to send them to magazines. She passed away before I finished this book but she is very much a part of many of the poems. And lastly thank you to my mother, Adchara — you are a magical mother and human. Thank you for showing me how to fall in love with life and make the most of every day. You made my world beautiful. Lastly I thank God, for my life, for the people in it, for every quiet moment of inspiration, and for creating me with this beautiful ache to write.